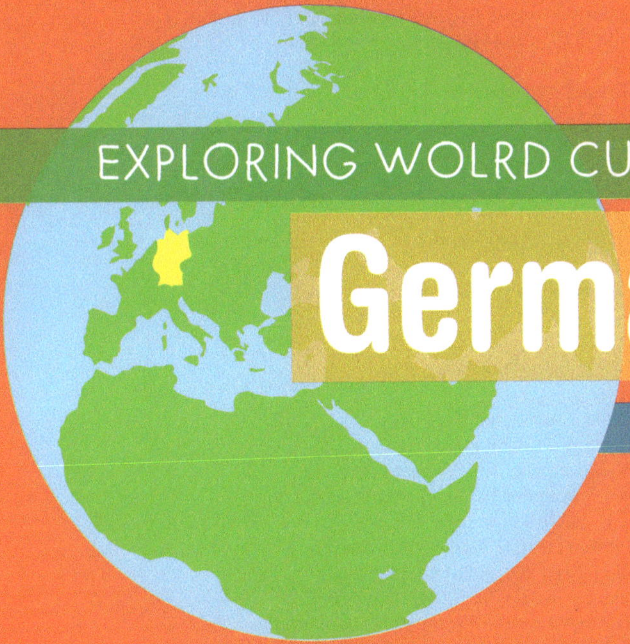

EXPLORING WOLRD CULTURES

Germany

Andrew Coddington

Cavendish Square
New York

Published in 2017 by Cavendish Square Publishing, LLC
243 5th Avenue, Suite 136, New York, NY 10016

First Edition

Library of Congress Cataloging-in-Publication Data

Names: Coddington, Andrew, author.
Title: Germany / Andrew Coddington.
Description: New York : Cavendish Square Pub., 2017. | Series: Exploring world cultures | Includes index. | Description based on print version record and CIP data provided by publisher; resource not viewed.
Identifiers: LCCN 2016001002 (print) | LCCN 2016000632 (ebook) | ISBN 9781502617392 (ebook) | ISBN 9781502618122 (pbk.) | ISBN 9781502618030 (library bound) | ISBN 9781502617910 (6 pack)
Subjects: LCSH: Germany--Juvenile literature.
Classification: LCC DD17 (print) | LCC DD17 .C64 2017 (ebook) | DDC 943--dc23
LC record available at http://lccn.loc.gov/2016001002

Editorial Director: David McNamara
Editor: Kristen Susienka
Copy Editor: Rebecca Rohan
Art Director: Jeffrey Talbot
Designer: Joseph Macri
Production Assistant: Karol Szymczuk
Photo Research: J8 Media

The photographs in this book are used by permission and through the courtesy of: Westend61/Getty Images, cover, 15; Sean Pavone/Shutterstock.com, 5; pavalena/Shutterstock.com, 6; Danita Delimont/Gallo Images/Getty Images, 7; DEA/G. Dagli Orti/De Agostini Picture Library/Getty Images, 8; Ewais/Shutterstock.com, 9; fhm/Moment/Getty Images, 10; T.J. Kirkpatrick/Getty Images, 11; ollo/iStock, 12; Lukassek/Shutterstock.com, 13; Guido Mieth/Moment Select/Getty Images, 16; Armin Weigel/picture-alliance/dpa/AP Images, 17; william87/iStock, 18; bbsferrari/iStock, 19; Mikhail Markovskiy/Shutterstock.com, 20; Look and Learn/Bridgeman Images, 21; Insights/Universal Images Group/Getty Images, 22; Jasmin Awad/iStock Editorial/Thinkstock, 24; Andreas Strauss/LOOK-foto/Getty Images, 26; VI Images/Getty Images, 27; Sean Gallup/Getty Images, 28.

Printed in the United States of America

Contents

Introduction

Germany is a special country. It has a long history, a **diverse** population, and good food.

At one time, Germany was a very violent place. In the 1900s, Germany fought in two World Wars. During World War II, the German army killed many innocent people. Today, it is a different place that welcomes many people.

Germany has an important place in the European Union (EU). The EU is a group of countries in Europe. They share the same money and political goals. Germany holds a lot of power in the EU.

Most people who live in Germany were born there. However, recently Germany has welcomed

refugees from the Middle East. Many refugees have escaped difficult times in their home countries, especially Libya, Iraq, and Syria.

Germany has a lot of customs and traditions. Learning about Germany can be fun!

Germany's Neuschwanstein Castle seems to be straight out of a storybook.

Geography

Germany sits almost in the center of Europe. It is not too big and not too small. It covers nearly 138,000 square miles (357,000 square kilometers).

Germany has a unique landscape. To the north are two seas. One is the North Sea (what Germans call *Nordsee*), and the other is the Baltic Sea (the *Ostee*). Germany also contains part of a

A map of Germany

FACT!

Germany is the seventh-largest country in Europe and the sixty-second-largest country in the world.

mountain range known as the Alps. There are three main rivers in Germany: the Rhine, the Danube, and the Elbe. Germany also has several forests.

Zugspitze is the highest point in the Bavarian Alps.

Germany's Climate

Germany has a moderate **climate**. It rarely gets very hot or very cold. Summers in Germany are usually between 70 and 80 degrees Fahrenheit (21 and 27 degrees Celsius). Winter temperatures can be 32°F (0°C) in the western part of Germany and well below freezing in the eastern part.

History

Germany has a complicated history. In ancient times, Germany had many tribes that fought each other. The Romans tried to conquer Germany, but they could not control all of it. Tribes still battled in the Middle Ages.

The ancient Romans and Germans battled each other for centuries.

From 1933 to 1945, Adolf Hitler led Germany. He wanted to control all of Europe. He also wanted Germany to be rid of people he thought were evil, especially the Jews. Hitler used the **Holocaust** to do this. He murdered millions of people during this time.

The Berlin Wall

When Germany lost World War II, the United States and the Soviet Union wanted to keep Germany from starting another war. They each took one half of the city of Berlin and built a wall to divide the city. Families and friends were separated. The Berlin Wall came down in 1989.

Today, parts of the Berlin Wall are decorated with art.

FACT!

The first early human fossil to be named was discovered in Germany in 1856 in the Neander Valley.

Government

The official name for Germany is the *Bundesrepublik Deutschland*, or the Federal **Republic** of Germany. The republic consists of sixteen states, called *Länder*. The Länder select the country's officials.

The Reichstag houses Germany's parliament.

There are three parts to Germany's government:

1) Parliament creates and passes laws, sets the budget, and decides how the country uses its military. It has two divisions, or houses: the Bundestag and the Bundesrat.

Chancellor Merkel

Angela Merkel is Germany's current chancellor. She was elected in 2005 and is the country's first female chancellor.

2) The executive branch of Germany includes the president and the chancellor. The president represents the state's interests. The chancellor acts as the head of the state and appoints ministers.

3) Germany's judiciary determines whether the laws passed by the legislature are constitutional.

FACT!

There are 630 members in the Bundestag. They meet in Berlin, the country's capital.

The Economy

Germany has a powerful **economy**. It is Europe's largest economy and the world's fifth largest.

Germany is known for its luxury cars.

Few Germans work in farming. The country has successful industries in other areas, such as banking, finance, and manufacturing. Germans make many different goods, including chemicals, machines, tools, electronics, and ships.

FACT!

Germany produces the third-most cars in the world after China and Japan. Germans make about three million cars each year!

Clean Energy

A clean solar power plant in Germany

Germany used to rely on nuclear power for most of its energy needs. That changed in 2011 when a nuclear plant in Japan had a meltdown. In 2011, Chancellor Angela Merkel said that all of the country's seventeen plants would close by 2022. Germany hopes to replace these plants with clean, renewable energies, such as wind and solar.

Germany may be most famous for its cars. Many of the world's top car brands are German. Mercedes-Benz, BMW, Audi, and Porsche have headquarters in Germany.

The Environment

Germany has not always treated the environment well. In 1985, Germany had the worst pollution of all European countries. Fortunately, Germany is changing that. Germany understands the risks posed by global **climate change**. Climate change is caused by "greenhouse gases," such as carbon dioxide, which is released by cars. These gases get caught in the atmosphere and cause the Earth to warm up.

FACT!

Between 1990 and 2005, Germany reduced the amount of greenhouse gases it released by 18 percent. During that same period, the United States released 16 percent more greenhouse gases.

The government has created laws meant to protect the environment. One law taxes the amount of greenhouse gases a person releases into the atmosphere.

Germany Recycles!

Germans take recycling very seriously. Homes have several different recycling bins. These are color coded to match what goes in them. Germans recycle nearly everything—papers, metals, plastics, and even old food!

Most houses in Germany have several different recycling bins.

The People Today

Germany has nearly 81 million people. It has the most people of all the countries of Europe and is the seventeenth most populous country in the world.

Germany is the most populous country in Europe.

FACT!

After World War I, so many men had been killed on the battlefield that only one in three women could find a husband.

Most people who live in Germany today were born there. Over 90 percent of Germany's population is German. However, there are more than just German people living there. There are also many immigrants living in Germany. The largest immigrant group comes from Turkey. Other immigrants in Germany come from Greece, Poland, Italy, and Russia.

Welcome Refugees

Germany has become home to thousands of refugees from Syria. These people are fleeing their homeland, where a deadly civil war has broken out. Just days after Chancellor Merkel announced refugees would be welcome in Germany, fifty thousand people were admitted into the country.

This Syrian family has found peace in Germany.

Lifestyle

A bustling shopping center in Cologne, Germany

Three-quarters of Germany's population live in cities. Germany's capital, Berlin, has the most people at 3.56 million.

Most Germans live a comfortable lifestyle. Over half of all Germans own cars, for example.

FACT!

Most German homes and apartments do not come with kitchen sinks, appliances, or even light fixtures.

Germans are known for being very polite, clean, and orderly. This is reflected in their daily life. German parks, streets, and towns are all carefully maintained. Many neighborhoods have a lot of rules about what people can and cannot do on certain days.

Shh! Quiet Time!

Many German towns are clean, quiet, and picturesque.

Many German towns enforce a *Ruhezeiten*, or quiet time. This time usually begins in the evening and lasts through early morning. During quiet time, people may not use tools or listen to music that might disturb their neighbors. In some places, a crying baby or even flushing a toilet may violate quiet time.

Religion

There are many religions in Germany. Some Germans are Jewish, others are Muslim, and others believe in different religions or no religion. About 70 percent of Germans are Christian. Half of German Christians are Roman Catholic. The other half are **Protestant**.

The cathedral in Cologne

FACT!

There are plans to build a "House of One" in Berlin. This space would give Christians, Jews, and Muslims one place to worship.

Protestantism began in Germany many centuries ago. In 1517, a German monk named Martin Luther grew angry with the Catholic Church. He published a paper called "The 95 Theses." In it, he talked about the bad things the church was doing. A new kind of Christianity called Protestantism started because of Martin Luther's actions.

German monk Martin Luther started Protestantism.

Christianity and Islam

Christians are the majority in Germany, but their numbers are shrinking. Many Christian Germans have stopped going to church. Meanwhile, the number of Muslims in the country is growing, thanks to immigration.

Language

Luther's Bible is the foundation for modern German.

The official language of Germany is German. There were once many versions of German. In the sixteenth century, Martin Luther translated the Christian Bible from Latin into German. Luther's German came from a part of Germany called Saxony. Luther's Bible became very common throughout Germany. The version of German he used became the modern German spoken today.

One Long Word!

Many German words are very long. This is because many words are put together into one word. Policeman is an example of a long word in English. One German word is *Rechtsschutzversicherungsgesellschaften*. At thirty-nine letters long, it was given a Guinness World Record!

Germany is not the only place where German is spoken. German is also the official language of Austria and Lichtenstein. Many people in Switzerland and Luxembourg speak it, too.

FACT!

German is the most commonly spoken language in Europe.

Arts and Festivals

Germans celebrate holidays with colorful carnivals.

Germany is known as the Land of Poets and Thinkers. For centuries, Germany has been the home of several well-known writers, philosophers, composers, architects, and other artists. Some famous Germans include Albrecht Dürer, Johann Sebastian Bach, Albert Einstein, and Anne Frank.

FACT!

Many Christmas traditions started in Germany, including Advent wreaths, Christmas pageants, and decorated evergreen trees.

Germany hosts many fun festivals every year. Popular festivals are Karneval and Oktoberfest. Karneval happens in the spring. It is also known as *Fastnacht* or *Fasching*. This festival is similar to Mardi Gras in New Orleans and takes place in the weeks before Lent. At Oktoberfest, many tourists visit to drink special German beer.

Famous Composers

In a *New York Times* ranking of history's top ten greatest composers, four were German. Of those four, Beethoven and Bach were listed as the top two.

Fun and Play

Many Germans play sports and attend concerts in big cities. Popular bands visit Germany every year.

Nearly 28 million Germans are members of a sporting club. Millions more play individually. Germans play many sports. Tennis and golf are very popular. Many Germans also participate in motor sports, such as car racing. The most popular car-racing sport is Formula One racing.

Alpine skiing is a popular pastime in Germany.

FACT!

The game Chinese checkers was actually invented in Germany!

In winter, Germans enjoy playing ice hockey. Germany has had a professional hockey league since 1948. Germans also make use of their many snow-covered mountains. Many Germans travel to German resorts to ski or snowboard.

Ja, Fußball!

The most popular sport in Germany is football, or soccer. Football in Germany is supported by the *Bundesliga*, or national league. Germany's national team has played in the FIFA World Cup many times. Germany won the World Cup in 2014.

Germany celebrates its 2014 World Cup win.

Food

If there's one food Germans love, it's sausage!

Traditional German food is hearty and delicious. Germans enjoy soft *brezel* (pretzels) with mustard, *kartoffelpuffer* (potato pancakes) with applesauce, savory *sauerbraten* (pot roast), and breaded meat called schnitzel.

The most popular German food is *wurst*, or sausage. It is served everywhere, from homes to

Oktoberfest

One of Germany's most famous festivals celebrates eating and drinking like no other in the world. For fifteen days every October, Germans in the city of Munich celebrate Oktoberfest. More than six million people come from around the world to enjoy drinking German beer, eat roasted chicken legs and sausage, and have a great time!

restaurants to street carts. Sausage is often served with shredded cabbage called sauerkraut.

A popular German dessert is *apfelstrudel* (apple strudel), a pastry filled with apples, sugar, and cinnamon. Apple strudel is served in warm, flaky slices.

FACT!

There are 1,500 varieties of German sausage!

Glossary

climate The weather of a certain area.

climate change A worldwide trend of warming temperatures.

diverse Made up of different cultures, beliefs, and people.

economy The ability of a country to make and buy goods.

Holocaust The mass murder of Jews under Adolf Hitler.

Protestant A type of Christianity that began in protest of the Catholic Church.

refugee Someone who travels to another country to escape violence in their own.

republic A government where people elect their officials.

Find Out More

Books

Egert-Romanowska, Joanna, and Malgorzata Omilanowska. *Germany*. DK Eyewitness Travel Guide. London: Dorling Kindersley Limited, 2014.

Heiman, Sarah. *Germany ABCs: A Book About the People and Places of Germany*. North Mankato, MN: Picture Window Books, 2002.

Website

Germany: Time for Kids

www.timeforkids.com/destination/germany

Video

Discover Germany

www.dw.com/en/program/discover-germany/s-7856-9798

Explore some of Germany's most famous historical sites up close!

Index

About the Author

Andrew Coddington has written many books for Cavendish Square Publishing. He loves to read about world history and cultures and, better yet, experience them firsthand through travel. He lives in Lancaster, New York, with his fiancée and dog.